SABERTOOTH

PATRICK O'BRIEN

Henry Holt and Company • New York

THERE ARE MANY kinds of cats in the world today.

There are lions on the savanna . . .

and jaguars
in the jungle.

There are cougars hunting in the mountains . . .

and house cats sleeping on sofas.

All are expert hunters with sharp claws and pointy teeth. But long ago there lived a big cat whose giant teeth would make today's cats look tame.

SABERTOOTH!

Sabertooths were ferocious hunters with two huge teeth that hung from their mouths like knives—perfect for biting through the thick, hairy hide of big beasts, such as mammoths and buffalo.

There were many kinds of sabertooths.

There was *Machairodus* (13 to 2 million years ago) . . .

and *Dinofelis* (5 to 1 million years ago).

There was *Megantereon* (3 to 2 million years ago) . . .

and *Homotherium* (3 million to 10,000 years ago).

But the best-known saber-toothed cat was *Smilodon* (3 million to 10,000 years ago).

Everything we know about saber-toothed cats comes from studying their fossilized remains. *Smilodon* skeletons show us that the ancient cats were about the same size as lions are today, but their bones were thicker and stronger than lions' bones are.

SMILODON SKELETON

very short tail

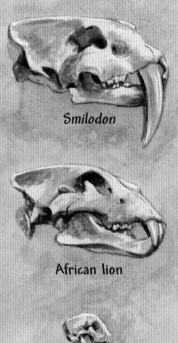

SKULLS

Smilodon

African lion

house cat

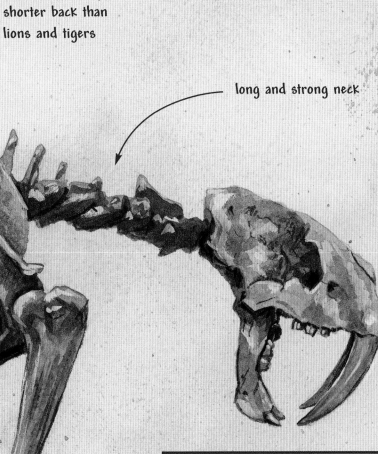

shorter back than
lions and tigers

long and strong neck

front legs and
shoulders were
heavy and strong

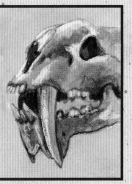

The sabertooth *Megantereon*
had a "flange" on its jawbone
that protected the giant teeth
from breaking.

A sabertooth
had to open
its jaw very,
very wide to
be able to use
its long fangs.

The long teeth of the saber-toothed cats are "canine" teeth. Most meat-eating mammals have canines. They often look like fangs. But saber-toothed cats' canines were some of the most dangerous weapons in the animal world. This picture shows an actual-size canine tooth from a South American *Smilodon*. It's about 11 inches long, but about five inches of it was inside the cat's skull.

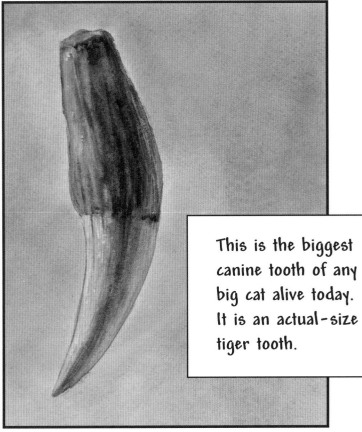

This is the biggest canine tooth of any big cat alive today. It is an actual-size tiger tooth.

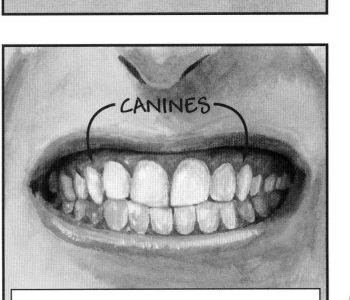

CANINES

People have canine teeth, too. They are sometimes a little sharp!

Saber-toothed cats were named for their long canine teeth, which look a bit like a curved sword called a saber.

MACHAIRODUS
13 to 2 million years ago

This is a family tree of cats. It shows how all cats evolved from the earliest cat, which lived more than 30 million years ago. About 20 million years ago the tree split into two kinds of cats. One kind evolved to become the sabertooths. They have all died out. The other kind evolved into all the cats that live today.

PROAILURUS
30 to 20 million years ago

PSEUDAELURUS
21 to 10 million years ago

Today's cats are not descended from sabertooths, but they are related to them. Modern cats are more like distant cousins to sabertooths than like great-great-grandchildren.

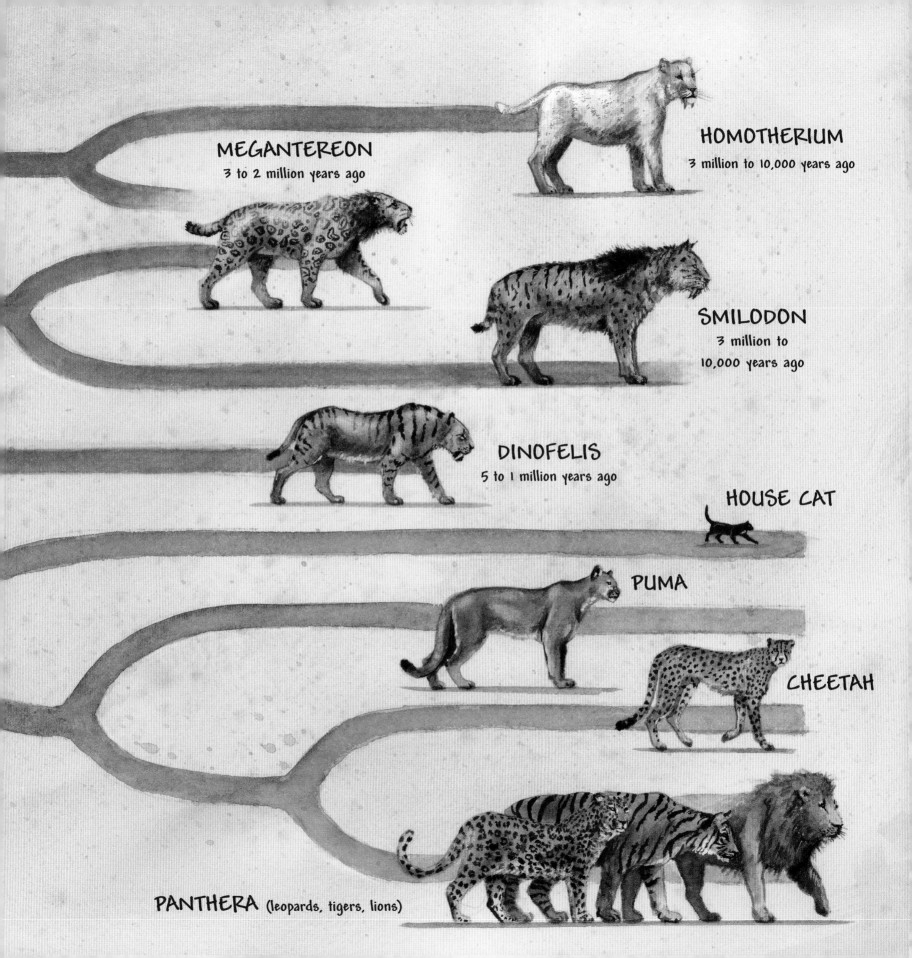

MEGANTEREON
3 to 2 million years ago

HOMOTHERIUM
3 million to 10,000 years ago

SMILODON
3 million to
10,000 years ago

DINOFELIS
5 to 1 million years ago

HOUSE CAT

PUMA

CHEETAH

PANTHERA (leopards, tigers, lions)

No one knows what color saber-toothed cats' fur was. No one knows what kind of patterns they might have had. But we can make some good guesses based on cats that live today.

Perhaps *Smilodon* looked like this . . .

or this . . .

or this.

Some *Homotheriums* lived in what is now Alaska. Perhaps they were white, like polar bears and arctic foxes.

Some sabertooths might even have been black, like black jaguars and leopards today.

Smilodons were heavy and strong, more like wrestlers than long-distance runners, so they probably couldn't catch a big animal in a long chase. But if they could sneak close enough to pounce, they could wrestle a really big animal to the ground and deliver a huge bite.

Smilodons may have helped each other in the hunt. Perhaps some of them chased their big prey toward others hiding in the underbrush, who would then spring out and attack the unlucky creature.

There were a few other ancient animals that also had saberlike teeth.

Barbourofelis was not a cat but a nimravid. Nimravids were fierce meat-eating mammals that have all died out.

Thylacosmilus was a marsupial. It was more closely related to kangaroos and opossums than to cats.

Both of these predators evolved separately from cats, but they both developed the same kind of huge teeth that saber-toothed cats did. This is because they hunted the same type of large animals as saber-toothed cats. They needed the big teeth to bring down their big prey.

Saber-toothed cats had to compete with many other ancient predators for a meal.

There was the short-faced bear . . .

and the cave-lion.

And there were strange hunters called creodonts . . .

and bear-dogs.

There was even a huge, ferocious bird called *Diatryma* that was about 7 feet tall.

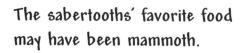
The sabertooths' favorite food may have been mammoth.

But a hungry sabertooth could also choose from hairy rhinos with huge horns . . .

and giant rodents that were bigger than cows.

Perhaps they preferred *Glyptodon*, a kind of armadillo that was built like a walking tank . . .

or *Dinohyus*, a strange, scary pig.

Sabertooths probably had a taste for ancient humans as well.

The sabertooth *Homotherium* lived in ancient Africa along with an extinct human species called *Homo erectus*. The big cat was stronger and faster, but *Homo erectus* was much smarter. If he got the chance, he could use fire or a weapon to fight off the savage beast.

Early Indians in the American West probably had many close encounters with *Smilodons*.

In what is now downtown Los Angeles, California, hungry *Smilodons* had a nasty surprise waiting for them.

Pools of sticky black tar formed deadly traps for ancient animals in a place now called the La Brea Tar Pits. Often the tar was covered with leaves and sticks, or even water, so the animals didn't see it. When a big mammal, like a bison or a mammoth, walked through the tar, its feet got stuck in the oily ooze and it began to slowly sink into the pit.

   The struggling animal attracted *Smilodons* looking for an easy meal. Then the *Smilodons* got stuck also, and all the animals sank together into the tar.

layer of water

For tens of thousands of years the tar pits trapped any animal unlucky enough to wander into them. The bones of those animals are still stuck deep in the tar.

tar seeps up from deep underground

For the last hundred years, scientists have been digging in the pits and bringing up bones. So far they have found the bones of more than 2,000 *Smilodons* who died in the pits. They have also found remains from lots of other animals, including birds, reptiles, amphibians, fish, and even bugs.

Smilodons died out about 10,000 years ago. At about the same time, many other large animals also became extinct. No one really knows why, but scientists have some ideas.

The world was getting warmer at that time, and this caused big changes in the environment. Some scientists think that the really large animals just couldn't adjust and went extinct. Once the large animals were gone, perhaps the Smilodons couldn't catch enough to eat. As their food died out, so did the Smilodons.

Some of the big cats still alive today are in danger of vanishing as well. Many of the wild places where they live are being destroyed to make room for the growing number of people on our planet. Unless humans take steps to protect these amazing creatures, perhaps the lions on the savanna and the jaguars in the jungle will one day go the way of the *Smilodons*, and only their bones will remain.

TO MOLLY O'BRIEN, WITH LOVE AND GRATITUDE

Henry Holt and Company, LLC
Publishers since 1866
175 Fifth Avenue
New York, New York 10010
www.HenryHoltKids.com

Henry Holt® is a registered trademark of Henry Holt and Company, LLC.
Copyright © 2008 by Patrick O'Brien
All rights reserved.
Distributed in Canada by H. B. Fenn and Company Ltd.

Library of Congress Cataloging-in-Publication Data
O'Brien, Patrick.
Sabertooth / Patrick O'Brien.—1st ed.
p.   cm.
ISBN-13: 978-0-8050-7105-4
ISBN-10: 0-8050-7105-9
1. Saber-toothed tigers—Juvenile literature. 2. Smilodon—Juvenile literature.
3. Dinosaurs—Extinction—Juvenile literature. I. Title.
QE882.C15O27 2008   569'.74—dc22   2007002792

First Edition—2008 / Book designed by JRS Design
The artist used watercolor and gouache on watercolor paper to create the illustrations for this book.
Printed in China on acid-free paper. ∞

1   3   5   7   9   10   8   6   4   2